PRE-SCHOOL NUMBERS 1-10

Fun-filled Activities

An imprint of Om Books International

1

one

Find and circle all the number 1s.

		2	1
		1	5
		3	1
1	5	1	1
3	1	2	2
1	2	1	4
2	1	3	5
3	2	1	1

Which hen has a basket with 1 ? Tick (✓) 1 .

Trace the number.

 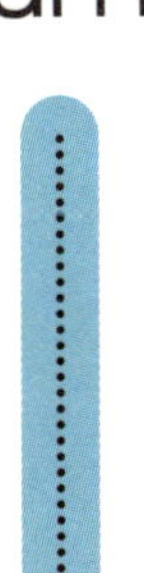    

2
two

Find and circle (O) all the number 2s.

Colour the pot with 2 fish.

Trace the number.

2 2 2 2 2 2

3
three

Find and circle (O) all the number 3s.

Circle ◯ the pot with 3 🌸.

Trace the number.

3 3 3 3 3 3

Count the stars, colour the correct number of circles and trace the correct number.

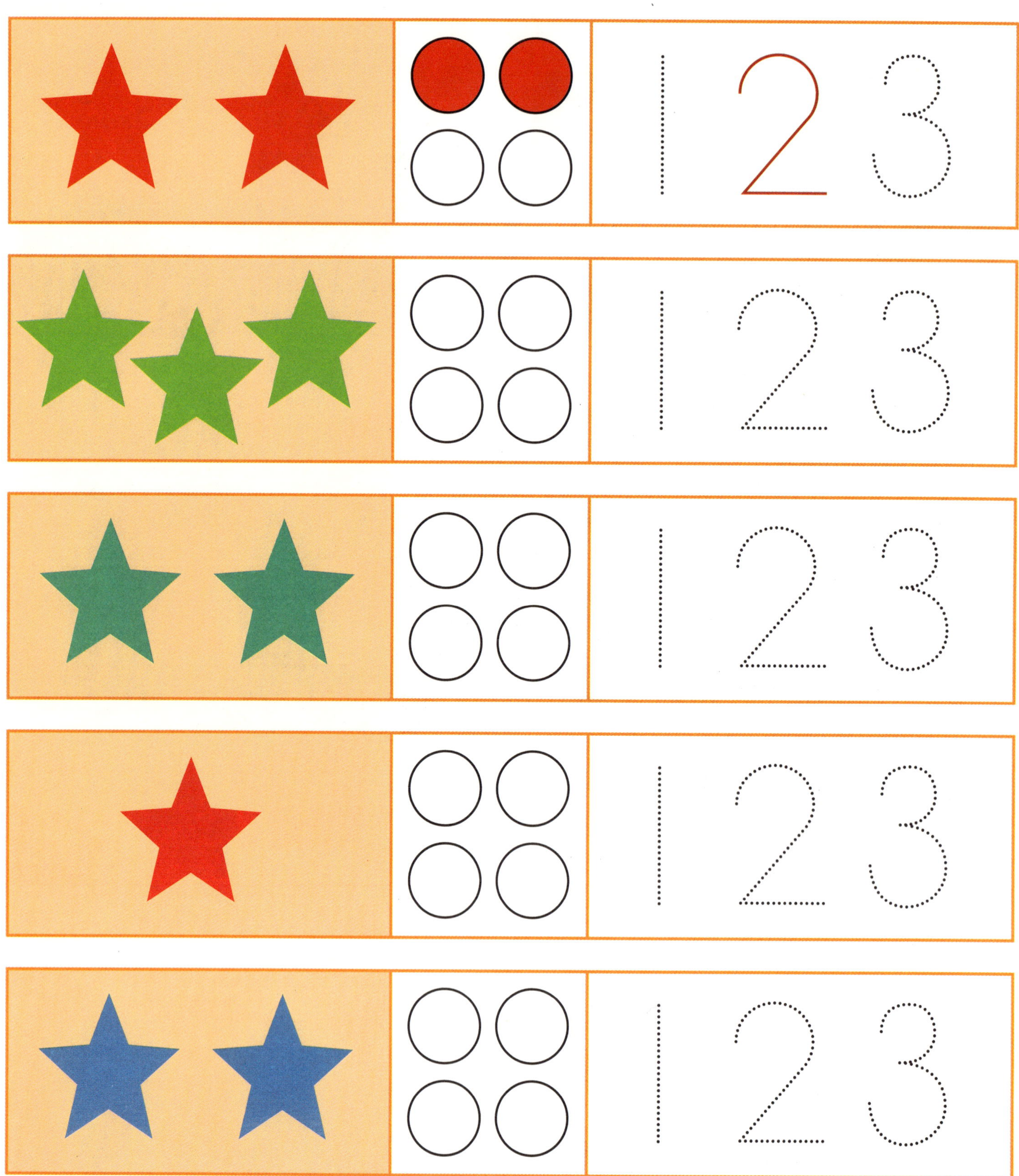

4
four

Find and circle (O) all the number 4s.

Circle ◯ the jar with 4 🍭.

Trace the number.

5
five

Find and circle (O) all the number 5s.

The bear wants 🧢 for his friends. Find and tick 5 🧢 from the picture.

Trace the number.

5 5 5 5 5 5

Count how many and circle (O) the correct number.

Trace the numbers and colour the correct number of things in each row.

1	
2	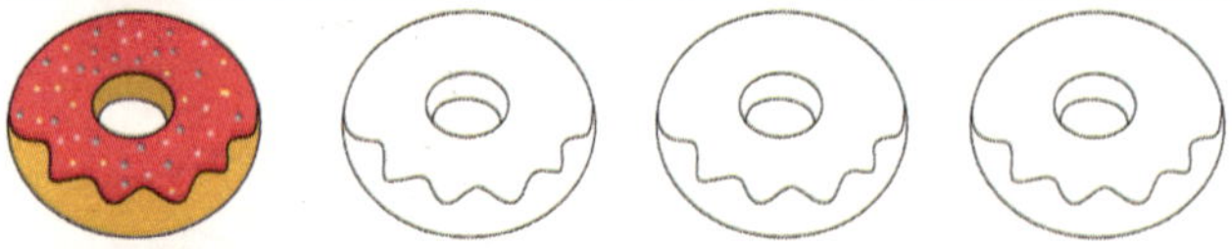
3	
4	
5	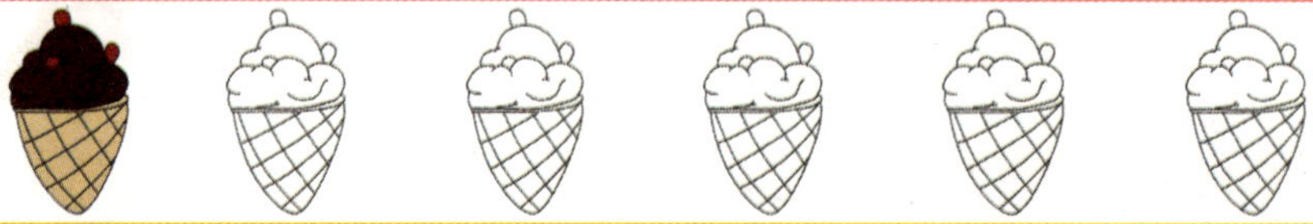

Count the items and circle (O) the correct number.

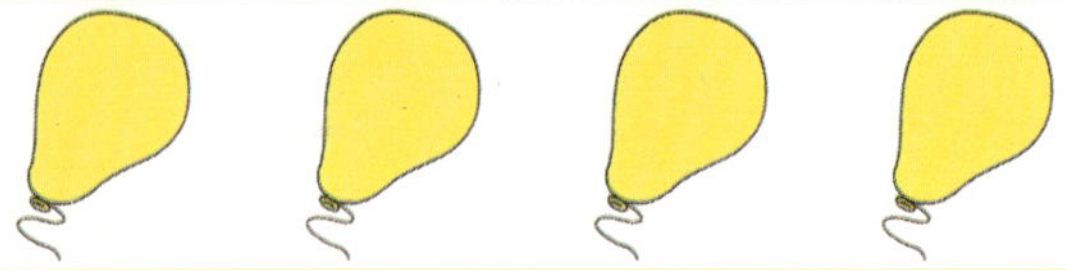	3	2	4
	1	2	5
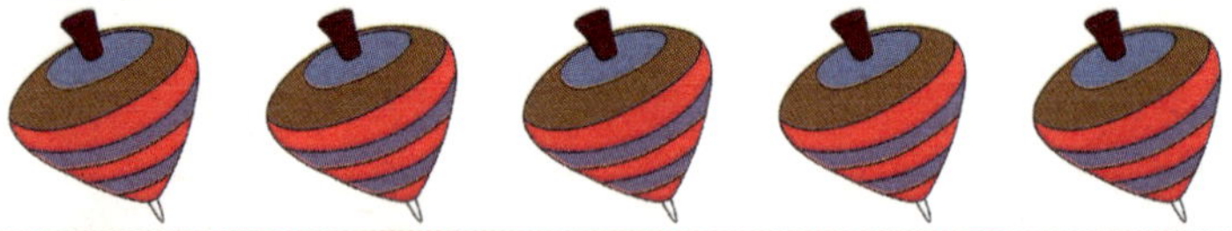	5	3	4
	1	3	2
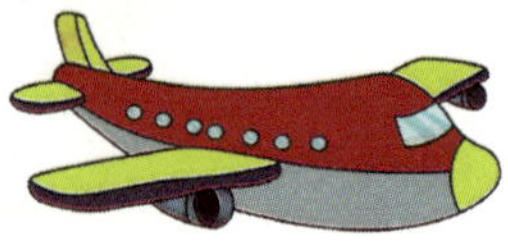	4	1	5

The children are playing 'I spy'. Help them. You have to:

Circle (O) 1

Cross (×) 2 

Tick (✓) 3 

Cross (×) 4

Circle (O) 5

6
six

Find and circle (O) all the number 6s.

Help the ant find its food. Draw a line by the correct path from the ant to the 6 .

Trace the number.

7
seven

Find and circle (O) all the number 7s.

7 are hiding in the picture. Can you find and put a X on them?

7		7	5
		5	6
		6	7
7	5	6	6
4	7	4	7
7	5	6	5
7	6	7	6
6	7	6	7

Trace the number.

7 7 7 7 7 7

8
Eight

Find and circle (O) all the number 8s.

		8	6
		7	8
		6	7
8	6	8	6
4	8	4	7
8	6	5	8
6	7	5	6
6	8	7	8

Trace the number.

Count the things in the box and colour the correct number of circles. Then trace the correct number.

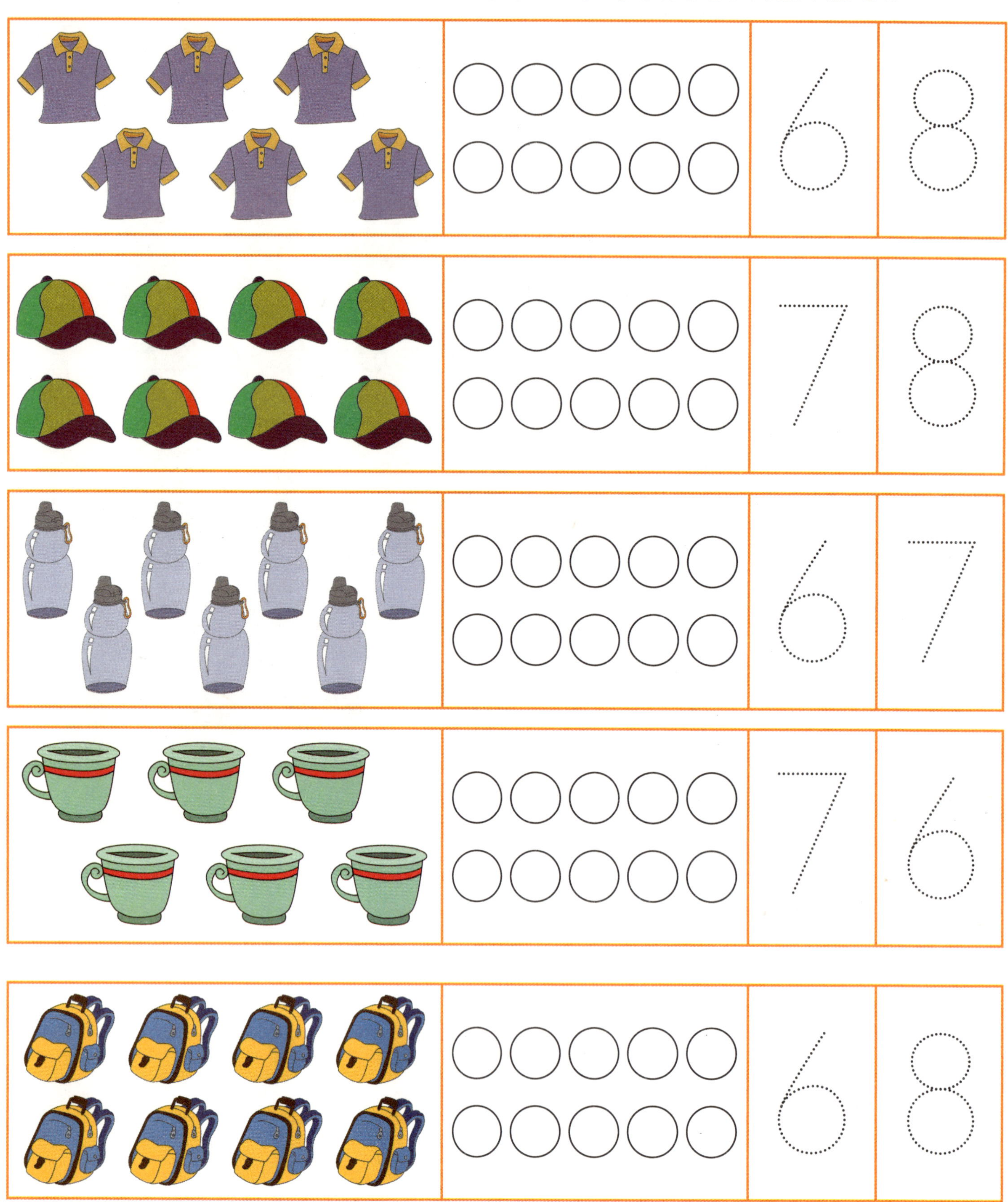

Count and write the correct number of objects that you see in the picture.

bags ______ racquets ______ shoes ______

crayons ____ balls ____

9

Nine

Find and circle (O) all the number 9s.

Help the Birdie pick 9 . Circle the 9 .

		9	7
		7	8
		8	9
9	7	8	9
7	8	9	7
8	9	7	8
9	7	8	9
7	9	7	9

Trace the number.

10
ten

Find and circle (O) all the number 10s.

Put a tick (✓) on 10 shell.

Trace the number.

Help the squirrel match the correct numbers by drawing lines.

Count the number of things in each box. Then trace over the correct number.

Practise all your numbers! Trace, write and count the numbers. One, two, three… go.

1	1	1	1
2	2	2	2
3	3	3	3
4	4	4	4
5	5	5	5
6	6	6	6
7	7	7	7
8	8	8	8
9	9	9	9
10	10	10	10

Answer key

Page 3

Page 10

Page 15

Page 5

Page 12

Page 17

Page 7

Page 13

Page 19

Page 8

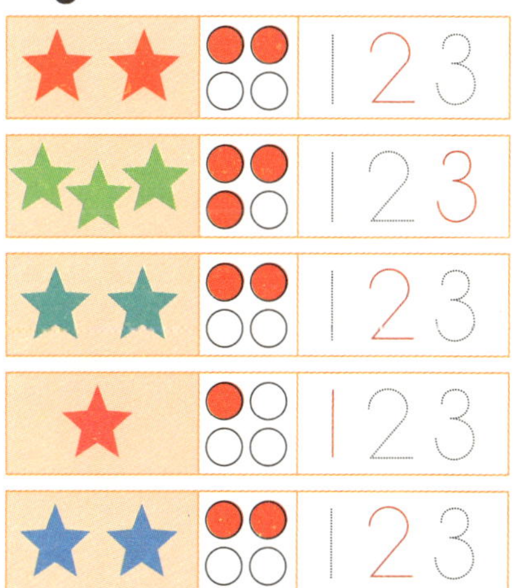

Page 14

Page 21

Answer key

Page 22

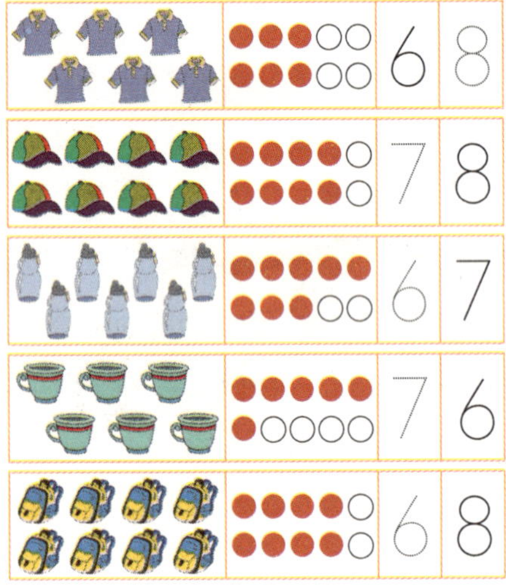

Page 28

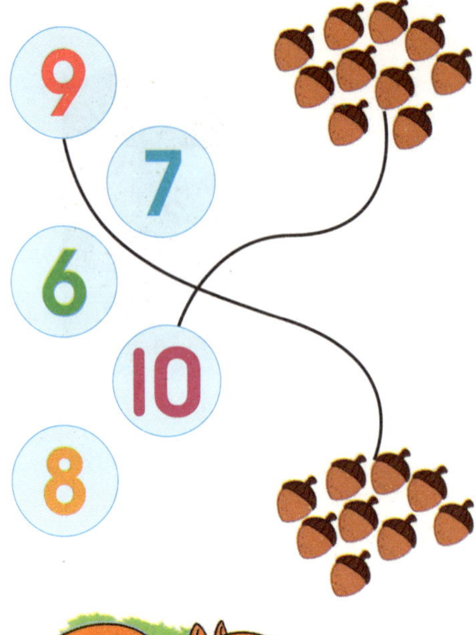

Page 23

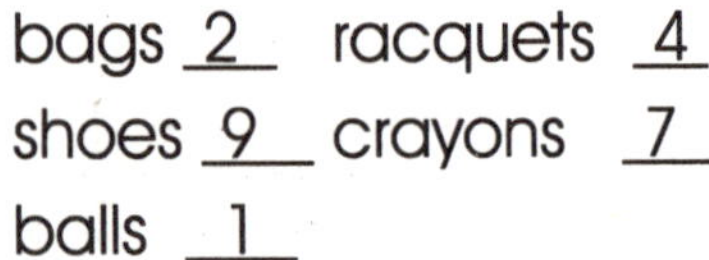

bags 2 racquets 4
shoes 9 crayons 7
balls 1

Page 25

Page 29

Page 27